TREASURY
OF
Poetry & Rhymes

This is a Parragon Publishing Book
This edition published in 2003
Parragon Publishing, Queen Street House, 4 Queen Street,
Bath, BA1 1HE, UK

Printed in China
ISBN 0 75257 690 9

Illustrated by
Kate Aldous, Claire Henley, Anna Cynthia Leplar,
Karen Perrins, Jane Tattersfield and Sara Walker
Jacket illustration by Diana Catchpole

TREASURY
OF
Poetry & Rhymes

p

LITTLE TREASURIES

CONTENTS

SIMPLE GIFTS

HURT NO LIVING THING

and

OTHER ANIMAL POEMS

HURT NO LIVING THING

Hurt no living thing,
  Ladybug nor butterfly,
Nor moth with dusty wing,
Nor cricket chirping cheerily,
Nor grasshopper, so light of leap,
  Nor dancing gnat,
  Nor beetle fat,
Nor harmless worms that creep.

CHRISTINA ROSSETTI

THE COW

The friendly cow all red and white,
  I love with all my heart:
She gives me cream with all her might,
  To eat with apple-tart.

She wanders lowing here and there,
  And yet she cannot stray,
All in the pleasant open air,
  The pleasant light of day;

And blown by all the winds that pass
  And wet with all the showers,
She walks among the meadow grass
  And eats the meadow flowers.

ROBERT LOUIS STEVENSON

THE FIELDMOUSE

Where the acorn tumbles down,
  There the ash tree sheds its berry,
With your fur so soft and brown,
  With your eye so round and merry,
Scarcely moving the long grass,
Fieldmouse, I can see you pass.

Little thing, in what dark den,
  Lie you all the winter sleeping?
Till warm weather comes again,
  Then once more I see you peeping
Round about the tall tree roots,
Nibbling at their fallen fruits.

Fieldmouse, fieldmouse, do not go,
  Where the farmer stacks his treasure,
Find the nut that falls below,
  Eat the acorn at your pleasure,
But you must not steal the grain
He has stacked with so much pain.

Make your hole where mosses spring,
  Underneath the tall oak's shadow,
Pretty, quiet, harmless thing,
  Play about the sunny meadow.
Keep away from corn and house,
None will harm you, little mouse.

CECIL FRANCES ALEXANDER

THE LAMB

Little lamb, who made thee?
Dost thou know who made thee?
Gave thee life, and bid thee feed
By the stream and o'er the mead;
Gave thee clothing of delight,
Softest clothing, woolly, bright;
Gave thee such a tender voice,
Making all the vales rejoice?
Little lamb, who made thee?
Dost thou know who made thee?

Little lamb, I'll tell thee,
Little lamb, I'll tell thee:
He is callèd by thy name,
For he calls himself a lamb.
He is meek, and he is mild;
He became a little child.
I a child, and thou a lamb,
We are callèd by his name.
Little lamb, God bless thee!
Little lamb, God bless thee!

WILLIAM BLAKE

19

CATERPILLAR

Brown and furry
Caterpillar in a hurry,
Take your walk
To the shady leaf, or stalk,
Or what not,
Which may be the chosen spot.
No toad spy you,
Hovering bird of prey pass by you;
Spin and die,
To live again a butterfly.

CHRISTINA ROSSETTI

THE CAT OF CATS

I am the cat of cats. I am
  The everlasting cat!
Cunning, and old, and sleek as jam,
  The everlasting cat!
I hunt the vermin in the night—
  The everlasting cat!
For I see best without the light—
  The everlasting cat!

WILLIAM BRIGHTY RANDS

DUCKS' DITTY

All along the backwater,
Through the rushes tall,
Ducks are a-dabbling.
Up tails all!

Ducks' tails, drakes' tails,
Yellow feet a-quiver,
Yellow bills all out of sight
Busy in the river!

Slushy green undergrowth
Where the roach swim—
Here we keep our larder,
Cool and full and dim.

Every one for what he likes!
We like to be
Heads down, tails up,
Dabbling free!

High in the blue above
Swifts whirl and call—

We are down a-dabbling
Up tails all!

KENNETH GRAHAME

MOTHER TABBYSKINS

Sitting at a window
In her cloak and hat
I saw Mother Tabbyskins,
The *real* old cat!
Very old, very old,
Crumplety and lame;
Teaching kittens how to scold—
Is it not a shame?

Kittens in the garden
Looking in her face,
Learning how to spit and swear—
Oh, what a disgrace!
Very wrong, very wrong,
Very wrong and bad;
Such a subject for our song,
Makes us all too sad.

Old Mother Tabbyskins,
  Sticking out her head,
Gave a howl, and then a yowl,
  Hobbled off to bed.
    Very sick, very sick,
      Very savage, too;
    Pray send for a doctor quick—
      Any one will do!

Doctor Mouse came creeping,
  Creeping to her bed;
Lanced her gums and felt her pulse,
  Whispered she was dead.
    Very sly, very sly,
      The *real* old cat
    Open kept her weather eye—
      Mouse! beware of that!

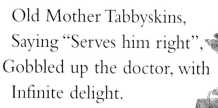

Old Mother Tabbyskins,
Saying "Serves him right",
Gobbled up the doctor, with
Infinite delight.
    Very fast, very fast,
    Very pleasant, too –
"What a pity it can't last!
    Bring another, do!"

ELIZABETH ANNA HART

26

EPIGRAM

*Engraved on the Collar of a Dog which I
Gave to His Royal Highness*

I am his Highness' Dog at Kew:
Pray tell me, sir, whose dog are you?

ALEXANDER POPE

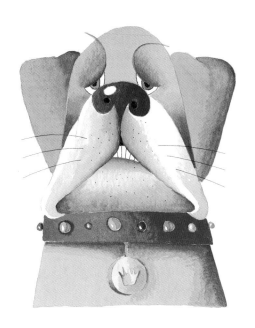

LITTLE TROTTY WAGTAIL

Little Trotty Wagtail, he went in the rain,
And twittering, tottering sideways, he ne'er
  got straight again;
He stooped to get a worm, and looked up to
  get a fly,
And then he flew away ere his feathers they
  were dry.

Little Trotty Wagtail, he waddled in the mud,
And left his little foot-marks, trample where
  he would.

He waddled in the water-pudge, and waggle
  went his tail,
And chirruped up his wings to dry upon
  the garden rail.

Little Trotty Wagtail, you nimble all about,
And in the dimpling water-pudge you waddle
  in and out;
Your home is nigh at hand and in the warm
  pig-sty;
So, little Master Wagtail, I'll bid you a good-bye.

JOHN CLARE

TWO LITTLE KITTENS

Two little kittens
One stormy night,
Began to quarrel,
And then to fight.

One had a mouse
And the other had none;
And that was the way
The quarrel begun.

"I'll have that mouse,"
Said the bigger cat.
"You'll have that mouse?
We'll see about that!"

"I will have that mouse,"
Said the tortoise-shell;
And, spitting and scratching,
On her sister she fell.

I've told you before
'Twas a stormy night,
When these two kittens
Began to fight.

The old woman took
The sweeping broom,
And swept them both
Right out of the room.

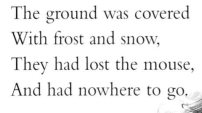

The ground was covered
With frost and snow,
They had lost the mouse,
And had nowhere to go.

So they lay and shivered
Beside the door,
Till the old woman
finished
Sweeping the floor.

And then they crept in
As quiet as mice,
All wet with snow
And as cold as ice.

They found it much better
That stormy night,
To lie by the fire,
Than to quarrel and fight.

JANE TAYLOR

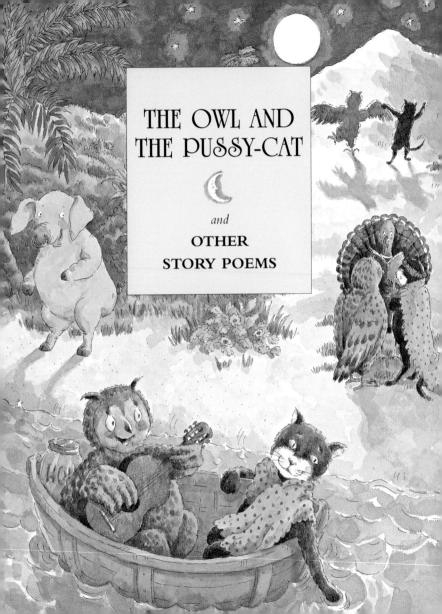

THE OWL AND THE PUSSY-CAT

and

OTHER STORY POEMS

THE OWL AND THE PUSSY-CAT

The Owl and the Pussy-Cat went to sea
  In a beautiful pea-green boat,
They took some honey, and plenty of money,
  Wrapped up in a five-pound note.
The Owl looked up to the stars above,
  And sang to a small guitar,
"O lovely Pussy! O Pussy, my love,
  What a beautiful Pussy you are,
      You are,
      You are,
  What a beautiful Pussy you are!"

Puss said to the Owl, "You elegant fowl!
  How charmingly sweet you sing!
O let us be married! too long we have tarried:
  But what shall we do for a ring?"
They sailed away for a year and a day,
  To the land where the Bong-tree grows,
And there in a wood a Piggy-wig stood,
  With a ring at the end of his nose,
        His nose,
        His nose,
  With a ring at the
        end of his nose.

"Dear Pig, are you willing to sell for one shilling,
Your ring?" Said the Piggy, "I will."
So they took it away, and were married next day
  By the Turkey who lived on the hill.
They dined on mince, and slices of quince,
  Which they ate with a runcible spoon:
And hand in hand, on the edge of the sand,
  They danced by the light of the moon,
      The moon,
      The moon,
  They danced by the light of the moon.

EDWARD LEAR

ELDORADO

Gaily bedight
A gallant knight,
In sunshine and in shadow,
Had journeyed long,
Singing a song,
In search of Eldorado.

But he grew old–
This knight so bold–
And o'er his heart a shadow
Fell as he found
No spot of ground
That looked like Eldorado.

37

And, as his strength
Failed him at length,
He met a pilgrim shadow:
"Shadow," said he,
"Where can it be,
This land of Eldorado?"

"Over the mountains
 Of the Moon,
Down the valley of the Shadow,
 Ride, boldly ride,"
 The shade replied,
"If you seek for Eldorado."

EDGAR ALLAN POE

THE WALRUS AND THE CARPENTER

The sun was shining on the sea
  Shining with all his might:
He did his very best to make
  The billows smooth and bright—
And this was odd, because it was
  The middle of the night.

The moon was shining sulkily,
  Because she thought the sun
Had got no business to be there
  After the day was done—
"It's very rude of him," she said,
  "To come and spoil the fun!"

The sea was wet as wet could be,
  The sands were dry as dry.
You could not see a cloud, because
  No cloud was in the sky:
No birds were flying overhead—
  There were no birds to fly.

The Walrus and the Carpenter
  Were walking close at hand;
They wept like anything to see
  Such quantities of sand:
"If this were only cleared away,"
  They said, "it would be grand!"

"If seven maids with seven mops
    Swept it for half a year,
Do you suppose," the Walrus said,
    "That they could get it clear?"
"I doubt it," said the Carpenter,
    And shed a bitter tear.

"O Oysters, come and walk with us!"
    The Walrus did beseech.
"A pleasant walk, a pleasant talk,
    Along the briny beach:
We cannot do with more than four,
    To give a hand to each."

The eldest Oyster looked at him,
  But never a word he said:
The eldest Oyster winked his eye,
  And shook his heavy head—
Meaning to say he did not choose
  To leave the oyster-bed.

But four young Oysters hurried up,
  All eager for the treat:
Their coats were brushed, their faces washed,
  Their shoes were clean and neat—
And this was odd, because, you know,
  They hadn't any feet.

Four other Oysters followed them,
  And yet another four;
And thick and fast they came at last,
  And more, and more, and more—
All hopping through the frothy waves,
  And scrambling to the shore.

The Walrus and the Carpenter
  Walked on a mile or so,
And then they rested on a rock
  Conveniently low:
And all the little Oysters stood
  And waited in a row.

"The time has come," the Walrus said,
  "To talk of many things:
Of shoes—and ships—and sealing-wax—
  Of cabbages—and kings—
And why the sea is boiling hot—
  And whether pigs have wings."

"But wait a bit," the Oysters cried,
  "Before we have our chat;
For some of us are out of breath,
  And all of us are fat!"
"No hurry!" said the carpenter.
  They thanked him much for that.

"A load of bread," the Walrus said,
    "Is what we chiefly need:
Pepper and vinegar besides
    Are very good indeed–
Now if you're ready, Oysters dear,
    We can begin to feed."

"But not on us!" the Oysters cried,
    Turning a little blue.
"After such kindness, that would be
    A dismal thing to do!"
"The night is fine," the Walrus said,
    "Do you admire the view?"

"It was so kind of you to come!
  And you are very nice!"
The Carpenter said nothing but
  "Cut us another slice:
I wish you were not quite so deaf—
  I've had to ask you twice!"

"It seems a shame," the Walrus said,
  "To play them such a trick,
After we've brought them out so far,
  And made them trot so quick!"
The Carpenter said nothing but
  "The butter's spread too thick!"

"I weep for you," the Walrus said:
  "I deeply sympathize."
With sobs and tears he sorted out
  Those of the largest size,
Holding his pocket-handkerchief
  Before his streaming eyes.

"O Oysters," said the Carpenter,
  "You've had a pleasant run!
Shall we be trotting home again?"
  But answer cam there none—
And this was scarcely odd, because
  They'd eaten every one.

LEWIS CARROLL

THE KANGAROO

Old Jumpety-Bumpety-Hop-and-Go-One
Was lying asleep on his side in the sun.
This old kangaroo, he was whisking the flies
(With his long glossy tail) from his ears and his eyes.
Jumpety-Bumpety-Hop-and-Go-One
Was lying asleep on his side in the sun,
Jumpety-Bumpety-Hop!

ANONYMOUS

AUSTRALIAN

HUMPTY DUMPTY'S POEM

In winter, when the fields are white,
I sing this song for your delight—

In spring, when woods are getting green,
I'll try and tell you what I mean.

In summer, when the days are long,
Perhaps you'll understand the song:

In autumn, when the leaves are brown,
Take pen and ink, and write it down.

I sent a message to the fish:
I told them "This is what I wish."

The little fishes of the sea,
They sent an answer back to me.

The little fishes' answer was
"We cannot do it, Sir, because—"

I sent to them again to say
"It will be better to obey."

The fishes answered with a grin,
"Why, what a temper you are in!"

I told them once, I told them twice:
They would not listen to advice.

I took a kettle large and new,
Fit for the deed I had to do.

My heart went hop, my heart went thump;
I filled the kettle at the pump.

Then someone came to me and said,
"The little fishes are in bed."

I said to him, I said it plain,
"Then you must wake them up again."

I said it very loud and clear;
I went and shouted in his ear.

But he was very stiff and proud;
He said "You needn't shout so loud!"

And he was very proud and stiff;
He said "I'd go and wake them, if–"

I took a corkscrew from the shelf:
I went to wake them up myself.

And when I found the door was locked,
I pulled and pushed and kicked and knocked.

And when I found the door was shut,
I tried to turn the handle, but–

LEWIS CARROLL

53

THE DUEL

The gingham dog and the calico cat
    Side by side on the table sat;
'Twas half-past twelve, and (what do you think!)
Nor one nor t'other had slept a wink!

    The old Dutch clock and the Chinese plate
    Appeared to know as sure as fate
There was going to be a terrible spat.
    (I wasn't there; I simply state
    What was told to me by the Chinese plate!)

Bow -

wow -

wow

The gingham dog went "Bow-wow-wow!"
And the calico cat replied "mee-ow!"
The air was littered, an hour or so,
With bits of gingham and calico,
  While the old Dutch clock in the chimney-place
  Up with its hands before its face,
For it always dreaded a family row!
  (Now mind: I'm only telling you
  What the old Dutch clock declares is true!)

Mee-ow

The Chinese plate looked very blue,
And wailed, "Oh, dear! what shall we do?"
But the gingham dog and the calico cat
Wallowed this way and tumbled that,
    Employing every tooth and claw
    In the awfullest way you ever saw—
And, oh! how the gingham and calico flew!
    (Don't fancy I exaggerate!
    I got my news from the Chinese plate!)

Next morning, where the two had sat,
They found no trace of dog or cat;
And some folks think unto this day
That burglars stole that pair away!
    But the truth about the cat and pup
    Is this: they ate each other up!
Now what do you really think of that!
    (The old Dutch clock it told me so,
    And that is how I came to know.)

EUGENE FIELD

ROLL OVER

There were ten in the bed
And the little one said:
  "Roll over! Roll over!"
So they all rolled over,
And one fell out.

There were nine in the bed
And the little one said:
  "Roll over! Roll over!"
So they all rolled over,
And one fell out.

There were eight in the bed
And the little one said:
  "Roll over, Roll over!"
So they all rolled over
And one fell out.

There were seven in the bed
And the little one said:
  "Roll over, Roll over!"
So they all rolled over,
And one fell out.

There were six in the bed
And the little one said;
  "Roll over! Roll over!"
So they all rolled over,
And one fell out.

There were five in the bed
And the little one said:
  "Roll over! Roll over!"
So they all rolled over,
And one fell out.

There were four in the bed
And the little one said:
 "Roll over! Roll over!"
So they all rolled over,
And one fell out.

There were three in the bed
And the little one said:
 "Roll over! Roll over!"
So they all rolled over,
And one fell out.

There were two in the bed
And the little one said:
  "Roll over! Roll over!"
So they all rolled over,
And one fell out.

There was one in the bed
And the little one said:
  "Roll over! Roll over!"
So HE rolled over,
And HE fell out.

So there was the bed—
And no one said:
  "Roll over! Roll over!"

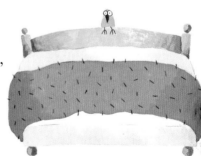

ANONYMOUS

ENGLISH

62

THE
WORLD

and

OTHER NATURE
POEMS

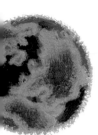

THE WORLD

Great, wide, beautiful, wonderful World,
With the wonderful water round you curled,
And the wonderful grass upon your breast–
World, you are beautifully dressed.

The wonderful air is over me,
And the wonderful wind is shaking the tree,
It walks on the water, and whirls the mills,
And talks to itself on the tops of the hills.

You friendly Earth, how far do you go,
With the wheatfields that nod and the rivers
  that flow,
With cities and gardens, and cliffs, and isles,
And people upon you for thousands of miles?

Ah, you are so great, and I am so small,
I tremble to think of you, World, at all;
And yet, when I said my prayers today,
A whisper inside me seemed to say,
"You are more than the Earth, though you are
  such a dot:
You can love and think, and the Earth cannot."

WILLIAM BRIGHTY RANDS

BLOW, BLOW, THOU
WINTER WIND

Blow, blow, thou Winter wind,
Thou art not so unkind
  As man's ingratitude;
Thy tooth is not so keen,
Because thou art not seen,
  Although thy breath be rude.
        Heigh ho! sing heigh ho! unto the
          green holly;
        Most friendship is feigning, most
          loving mere folly:
          Then heigh ho, the holly!
          This life is most jolly.

Freeze, freeze, thou bitter sky,
Thou dost not bite so nigh
  As benefits forgot;
Though thou the waters warp,
Thy sting is not so sharp
  As friend remembered not.
Heigh ho! sing heigh ho! unto the green holly;
Most friendship is feigning, most loving
    mere folly:
  Then heigh ho, the holly!
  This life is most jolly.

WILLIAM SHAKESPEARE

SPRING

Sound the Flute!
Now it's mute.
Birds delight
Day and Night;
Nightingale
In the dale,
Lark in Sky,
Merrily,
Merrily, Merrily, to welcome in the Year.

Little Boy,
Full of joy;
Little Girl,
Sweet and small;
Cock does crow,
So do you;
Merry voice,
Infant noise,
Merrily, Merrily, to welcome in the Year.

Little Lamb,
Here I am;
Come and lick
My white neck;

Let me pull
Your soft Wool;
Let me kiss
Your soft face;
Merrily, Merrily, we welcome in the Year.

WILLIAM BLAKE

THE DAYS ARE CLEAR

The days are clear,
   Day after day,
When April's here
   That leads to May,
And June
Must follow soon:
   Stay, June, stay!—
If only we could stop the moon
And June!

CHRISTINA ROSETTI

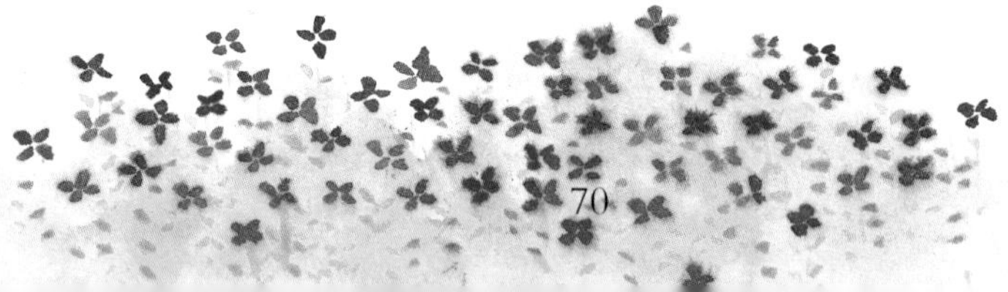

AUTUMN FIRES

In the other gardens
  And all up the vale,
From the autumn bonfires
  See the smoke trail!

Pleasant summer over
  And all the summer flowers,
The red fire blazes,
  The grey smoke towers.

Sing a song of seasons!
  Something bright in all!
Flowers in the summer,
  Fires in the fall!

ROBERT LOUIS STEVENSON

SNOW

In the gloom of whiteness,
In the great silence of snow,
A child was sighing
And bitterly saying: "Oh,
They have killed a white bird up there
   on her nest,
The down is fluttering from her breast!"
And still it fell through that dusky brightness
On the child crying for the bird of the snow.

EDWARD THOMAS

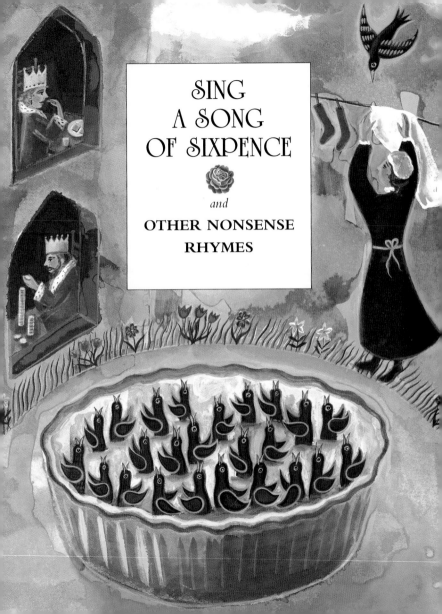

SING
A SONG
OF SIXPENCE

and

OTHER NONSENSE
RHYMES

SING A SONG OF SIXPENCE

Sing a song of sixpence,
  A pocket full of rye;
Four and twenty blackbirds,
  Baked in a pie.

When the pie was opened,
  The birds began to sing;
Was not that dainty dish,
  To set before the king?

The king was in his counting-house,
  Counting out his money;
The queen was in the parlor,
  Eating bread and honey.

The maid was in the garden,
  Hanging out the clothes,
There came a little blackbird,
  And snapped off her nose.

OVER THE HILLS AND FAR AWAY

When I was young and had no sense
I bought a fiddle for eighteen pence,
And the only tune that I could play
Was "Over the Hills and Far Away."

HEY, DIDDLE, DIDDLE

Hey, diddle, diddle, the cat and the fiddle,
  The cow jumped over the moon;
The little dog laughed to see such sport,
  And the dish ran away with the spoon!

HIGGLETY, PIGGLETY, POP!

Higglety, pigglety, pop!
The dog has eaten the mop;
The pig's in a hurry,
The cat's in a flurry,
Higglety, pigglety, pop!

WE'RE ALL IN THE DUMPS

We're all in the dumps,
  For diamonds and trumps,
The kittens are gone to St. Paul's,
  The babies are bit,
  The moon's in a fit,
And the houses are built without walls.

GOOSEY, GOOSEY, GANDER

Goosey, goosey, gander,
  Whither shall I wander,
Upstairs, and downstairs,
  And in my lady's chamber.
There I met an old man,
  Who would not say his prayers,
I took him by his left leg
  And threw him down the stairs.

DAFFY-DOWN-DILLY

Daffy-
  Down-
  Dilly
  has come
up to
  town

In a
  yellow
  petticoat
  and a
  green
  gown.

THE LION AND THE UNICORN

The lion and the unicorn
  Were fighting for the crown:
The lion beat the unicorn
  All round the town.
Some gave them white bread,
  Some gave them brown:
Some gave them plum-cake
  And drummed them out of town.

POP GOES THE WEASEL

Up and down the City Road
  In and out the Eagle,
That's the way the money goes,
  Pop goes the weasel!

Half a pound of tuppenny rice,
  Half a pound of treacle,
Mix it up and make it nice,
  Pop goes the weasel!

Every night when I go out
  The monkey's on the table;
Take a stick and knock it off,
  Pop goes the weasel!

ROBIN THE BOBBIN

Robin the Bobbin, the big-bellied Ben,
He ate more meat than fourscore men;
He ate a cow, he ate a calf,
He ate a butcher and a half;
He ate a church, he ate a steeple,
He ate the priest and all the people!
    A cow and a calf,
    An ox and a half,
    A church and a steeple,
    And all the good people,
And yet he complained that his
    stomach wasn't full.

HECTOR PROTECTOR

Hector Protector was dressed all in green;
Hector Protector was sent to the Queen.
The Queen did not like him,
No more did the King;
So Hector Protector was sent back again.

ONE, TWO, BUCKLE MY SHOE

One, two,
Buckle my shoe;
Three, four,
Shut the door;
Five, six,
Pick up sticks;
Seven, eight,
Lay them straight;
Nine, ten,
A good fat hen;

Eleven, twelve,
Who will delve?
Thirteen, fourteen,
Maids a-courting;
Fifteen, sixteen,
Maids a-kissing;
Seventeen, eighteen,
Maids a-waiting;
Nineteen, twenty,
My stomach's empty.

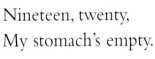

IF ALL THE SEAS WERE ONE SEA

If all the seas were one sea,
What a *great* sea that would be!
And if all the trees were one tree,
What a *great* tree that would be!
And if all the axes were one ax,
What a *great* ax that would be!
And if all the men were one man,
What a *great* man he would be!
And if the *great* man took the *great* ax,
And cut down the *great* tree,
And let it fall into the *great* sea,
What a splish splash *that* would be!

88

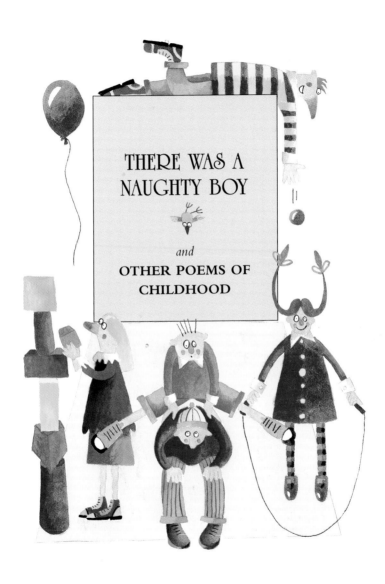

THERE WAS A NAUGHTY BOY

and

OTHER POEMS OF CHILDHOOD

THERE WAS A NAUGHTY BOY

There was a naughty boy,
　A naughty boy was he,
He would not stop at home,
　He could not quiet be—
　　He took
　　In his knapsack
　　A book
　　Full of vowels
　　And a shirt
　　With some towels,
　　A slight cap
　　For night cap,
　　A hair brush,
　　Comb ditto,
　　New stockings—
　　For old ones
　　Would split O!

This knapsack
    Tight at's back
    He rivetted close
And followed his nose
    To the North,
    To the North,
And followed his nose
    To the North.
        There was a naughty boy,
            And a naughty boy was he,
        He ran away to Scotland
            The people for to see—
            There he found
                That the ground
                Was as hard,
                    That a yard
                    Was as long,

That a song
Was as merry,
That a cherry
Was a red—
That lead
Was as weighty
That fourscore
Was as eighty,
That a door
Was as wooden
As in England—
So he stood in his shoes
    And he wondered,
    He wondered,
He stood in his shoes
    And he wondered.

JOHN KEATS

92

ALL THE BELLS WERE RINGING

All the bells were ringing,
And all the birds were singing,
When Molly sat down crying
  For her broken doll:
  O you silly Moll!
Sobbing and sighing
  For a broken doll,
When all the bells are ringing
And all the birds are singing.

LITTLE BOY BLUE

Little Boy Blue,
  Come blow your horn,
The sheep's in the meadow,
  The cow's in the corn.

Where is the boy
  Who looks after the sheep?
He's under a haycock
  Fast asleep.
Will you wake him?
  No, not I,
For if I do,
  He's sure to cry.

THERE WAS A LITTLE BOY

There was a little boy went into a barn,
  And lay down on some hay;
An owl came out and flew about,
  And the little boy ran away.

THE SWING

How do you like to go
up in a swing,
  Up in the air so blue?
Oh, I do think it the
pleasantest thing
  Ever a child can do!

Up in the air and over the wall,
  Till I can see so wide,
Rivers and trees and cattle and all
  Over the countryside—

Till I look down on the garden green,
  Down on the roof so brown—
Up in the air I go flying again,
  Up in the air and down!

ROBERT LOUIS STEVENSON

97

ANNA BANANA

Anna Banana
Played the piano;
The piano broke
And Anna choked.

LUCY LOCKET

Lucy Locket lost her pocket,
  Kitty Fisher found it,
But not a penny was there in it
  Just the binding round it

LITTLE MISS MUFFET

Little Miss Muffet
Sat on a tuffet,
Eating her curds and whey;
There came a great spider,
Who sat down beside her,
And frightened Miss Muffet away.

A GOOD PLAY

We built a ship upon the stairs
All made of the back-bedroom chairs,
And filled it full of sofa pillows
To go a-sailing on the billows.

We took a saw and several nails,
And water in the nursery pails;
And Tom said, "Let us also take
An apple and a slice of cake";
Which was enough for Tom and me
To go a-sailing on, till tea.

We sailed along for days and days,
And had the very best of plays;
But Tom fell out and hurt his knee,
So there was no one left but me.

ROBERT LOUIS STEVENSON

THE LITTLE DOLL

I once had a sweet little doll, dears,
  The prettiest doll in the world;
Her cheeks were so red and so white, dears,
  And her hair was so charmingly curled.
But I lost my poor little doll, dears,
  As I played in the heath one day;
And I cried for her more than a week, dears;
  But I never could find where she lay.

I found my poor little doll, dears,
    As I played in the heath one day:
Folks say she is terribly changed, dears,
    For her paint is all washed away,
And her arm trodden off by the cows, dears
    And her hair not the least bit curled:
Yet for old sakes' sake she is still, dears,
    The prettiest doll in the world.

CHARLES KINGSLEY

BROTHER AND SISTER

"Sister, sister go to bed!
Go and rest your weary head."
Thus the prudent brother said.

"Do you want a battered hide,
Or scratches to your face applied?"
Thus his sister calm replied.

"Sister, do not raise my wrath.
I'd make you into mutton broth
As easily as kill a moth!"

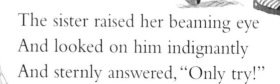

The sister raised her beaming eye
And looked on him indignantly
And sternly answered, "Only try!"

Off to the cook he quickly ran.
"Dear Cook, please lend a frying-pan
To me as quickly as you can."
"And wherefore should I lend it you?"
"The reason, Cook, is plain to view.
I wish to make an Irish stew."
"What meat is in that stew to go?"
"My sister'll be the contents!"
                    "Oh!"
"You'll lend the pan to me, Cook?"
                    "No!"

Moral: Never stew your sister.

LEWIS CARROLL

SKIPPING

Little children skip,
The rope so gaily gripping,
  Tom and Harry,
  Jane and Mary,
  Kate, Diana,
  Susan, Anna,
All are fond of skipping!

The grasshoppers all skip,
The early dew-drop sipping,
  Under, over
  Bent and clover,
  Daisy, sorrel,
  Without quarrel,
All are fond of skipping!

The little boats they skip,
Beside the heavy shipping,
  And while the squalling
  Winds are calling,
  Falling, rising,
  Rising, falling
All are fond of skipping!

The autumn leaves they skip,
When blasts the trees are stripping;
  Bounding, whirling,
  Sweeping, twirling,
  And in wanton
  Mazes curling,
All are fond of skipping!

THE CHILDREN'S HOUR

Between the dark and the daylight,
  When the night is beginning to lower,
Comes a pause in the day's occupations,
  That is known as the Children's Hour.

I hear in the chamber above me
  The patter of little feet,
The sound of a door that is opened,
  And voices soft and sweet.

From my study I see in the lamplight,
  Descending the broad hall stair,
Grave Alice, and laughing Allegra,
  And Edith with golden hair.

A whisper, and then a silence:
  Yet I know by their merry eyes
They are plotting and planning together
  To take me by surprise.

A sudden rush from the stairway,
  A sudden raid from the hall!
By three doors left unguarded
  They enter my castle wall!

They climb up into my turret
  O'er the arms and back of my chair;
If I try to escape, they surround me;
  They seem to be everywhere.

They almost devour me with kisses,
  Their arms about me entwine,
Till I think of the Bishop of Bingen
  In his Mouse-Tower on the Rhine!

Do you think, O blue-eyed banditti,
  Because you have scaled the wall,
Such an old mustache as I am
  Is not a match for you all!

I have you fast in my fortress,
 And will not let you depart,
But put you down into the dungeon
 In the round-tower of my heart.

And there will I keep you forever,
 Yes, forever and a day,
Till the walls shall crumble to ruin,
 And moulder in dust away!

HENRY WADSWORTH LONGFELLOW

GOING DOWN HILL ON A BICYCLE

With lifted feet, hands still,
I am poised, and down the hill
Dart, with heedful mind;
The air goes by in a wind.

Swifter and yet more swift,
Till the heart with a mighty lift
Makes the lungs laugh, the throat cry:–
"O bird, see; see, bird, I fly.

"Is this, is this your joy?
O bird, then I, though a boy,
For a golden moment share
Your feathery life in air!"

Say, heart, is there aught like this
In a world that is full of bliss?
'Tis more than skating, bound
Steel-shod to the level ground.

Speed slackens now, I float
Awhile in my airy boat;
Till, when the wheels scarce crawl,
My feet to the treadles fall.

Alas, that the longest hill
Must end in a vale; but still,
Who climbs with toil, wheresoe'er,
Shall find wings waiting there.

HENRY CHARLES BEECHING

HERE WE GO ROUND THE MULBERRY BUSH

Here we go round the mulberry bush,
The mulberry bush, the mulberry bush,
Here we go round the mulberry bush,
On a cold and frosty morning.

This is the way we wash our hands,
Wash our hands, wash our hands,
This is the way we wash our hands,
On a cold and frosty morning.

Here we go round the mulberry bush,
The mulberry bush, the mulberry bush,
Here we go round the mulberry bush,
On a cold and frosty morning.

This is the way we wash our clothes,
Wash our clothes, wash our clothes,
This is the way we wash our clothes,
On a cold and frosty morning.

Here we go round the mulberry bush,
The mulberry bush, the mulberry bush,
Here we go round the mulberry bush,
On a cold and frosty morning.

This is the way we go to school,
We go to school, we go to school,
This is the way we go to school,
On a cold and frosty morning.

Here we go round the mulberry bush,
The mulberry bush, the mulberry bush,
Here we go round the mulberry bush,
On a cold and frosty morning.

MINNIE AND MATTIE

Minnie and Mattie
  And fat little May,
Out in the country,
  Spending a day.

Such a bright day,
  With the sun glowing,
And the trees half in leaf,
  And the grass growing.

Pinky white pigling
  Squeals through his snout,
Woolly white lambkin
  Frisks all about.

Cluck! cluck! the nursing hen
  Summons her folk,—
Ducklings all downy soft,
  Yellow as yolk.

Cluck! cluck! the mother hen
  Summons her chickens
To peck the dainty bits
  Found in her pickings.

Minnie and Mattie
  And May carry posies,
Half of sweet violets,
  Half of primroses.

Give the sun time enough,
  Glowing and glowing,
He'll rouse the roses
  And bring them blowing.

Don't wait for roses
  Losing today,
O Minnie, Mattie,
  And wise little May.

Violets and primroses
  Blossom to-day
For Minnie and Mattie
  And fat little May.

CHRISTINA ROSSETTI

A BOY'S SONG

Where the pools are bright and deep,
Where the grey trout lies asleep,
Up the river and o'er the lea,
That's the way for Billy and me.

Where the blackbird sings the latest,
Where the hawthorn blooms the
     sweetest,
Where the nestlings chirp and flee,
That's the way for Billy and me.

Where the mowers mow the cleanest,
Where the hay lies thick and greenest;
There to trace the homeward bee,
That's the way for Billy and me.

Where the hazel bank is steepest,
Where the shadow falls the deepest,
Where the clustering nuts fall free,
That's the way for Billy and me.

Why the boys should drive away
Little sweet maidens from their play,
Or love the banter and fight so well,
That's the thing I never could tell.

119

But this I know, I love to play
Through the meadow, among
   the hay;
Up the water and o'er the lea,
That's the way for Billy and me.

JAMES HOGG

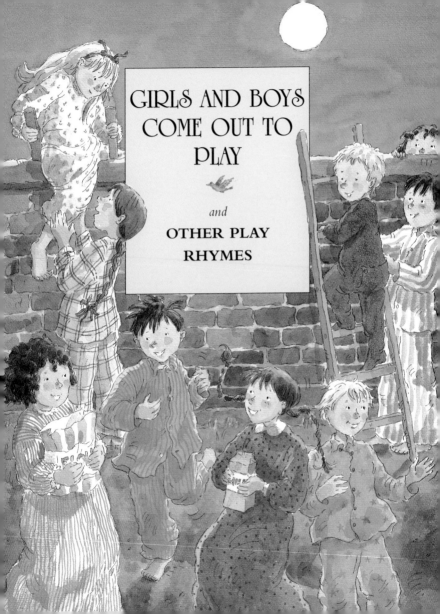

GIRLS AND BOYS COME OUT TO PLAY

and

OTHER PLAY RHYMES

GIRLS AND BOYS COME OUT TO PLAY

Girls and boys, come out to play;
The moon doth shine as bright as day;
Leave your supper, and leave your sleep,
And come with your playfellows into the street.
Come with a whoop, come with a call,
Come with a good will or not at all.
Up the ladder and down the wall,
A halfpenny loaf will serve us all.
You find milk, and I'll find flour,
And we'll have a pudding in half-an-hour.

GEORGIE, PORGIE

Georgie, Porgie, pudding and pie,
Kissed the girls and made them cry;
When the boys came out to play
Georgie Porgie ran away.

I SCREAM

I scream, you scream,
We all scream for ice cream!

LITTLE SALLY WATERS

Little Sally Waters,
Sitting in the sun,
Crying and weeping,
For a young man.
Rise, Sally, rise,
Dry your weeping eyes,
Fly to the east,
Fly to the west,
Fly to the one you love the best.

I REMEMBER, I REMEMBER

I remember, I remember
The house where I was born,
The little window where the sun
Came peeping in at morn;
He never came a wink too soon
Nor brought too long a day;
But now, I often wish the night
Had borne my breath away.

I remember, I remember
The roses, red and white,
The violets, and the lily-cups–
Those flowers made of light!
The lilacs where the robin built,
And where my brother set
The laburnum on his birthday–
The tree is living yet!

I remember, I remember
Where I was used to swing,
And thought the air must rush as fresh
To swallows on the wing;
My spirit flew in feathers then
That is so heavy now,
And summer pools could
        hardly cool
The fever on my brow.

I remember, I remember
The fir trees dark and high;
I used to think their slender tops
Were close against the sky:
It was a childish ignorance,
But now 'tis little joy
To know I'm farther off from Heaven
Than when I was a boy.

THOMAS HOOD

127

OLIVER TWIST

Oliver Twist
You can't do this,
So what's the use
Of trying?
Touch your toe,
Touch your knee,
Clap your hands,
Away we go.

A SAILOR WENT TO SEA

A sailor went to sea, sea, sea,
To see what he could see, see, see,
But all that he could see, see, see,
Was the bottom of the deep blue sea, sea, sea

HARK AT THE ROBBERS

Hark at the robbers going through,
  Through, through, through; through,
    through, through;
Hark at the robbers going through,
  My fair lady.

What have the robbers done to you,
  You, you, you; you, you, you?
What have the robbers done to you,
  My fair lady?

Stole my gold watch and chain,
    Chain, chain, chain; chain, chain, chain.
Stole my gold watch and chain,
    My fair lady.

How many pounds will set us free,
  Free, free, free; free, free, free?
How many pounds will set us free,
   My fair lady?

A hundred pounds will set you free,
  Free, free, free; free, free, free;
A hundred pounds will set you free,
   My fair lady.

We have not a hundred pounds,
  Pounds, pounds, pounds; pounds, pounds, pounds;
We have not a hundred pounds,
    My fair lady.

Then to prison you must go,
  Go, go, go; go, go, go;
Then to prison you must go,
    My fair lady.

To prison we will not go,
      Go, go, go; go, go, go;
  To prison we will not go,
        My fair lady.

SNEEZE ON MONDAY

Sneeze on Monday, sneeze for danger;
Sneeze on Tuesday, kiss a stranger;
Sneeze on Wednesday, get a letter;
Sneeze on Thursday, something better;
Sneeze on Friday, sneeze for sorrow;
Sneeze on Saturday, see your sweetheart
tomorrow.

RAIN, RAIN, GO AWAY

Rain, rain, go away,
Come again another day.

HAVE YOU SEEN THE MUFFIN MAN

Have you seen the muffin man, the muffin man,
  the muffin man,
Have you seen the muffin man that lives in Drury
  Lane O?
Yes, I've seen the muffin man, the muffin man,
  the muffin man;
Yes, I've seen the muffin
  man who lives in
  Drury Lane O.

A FARMYARD SONG

I had a cat and the cat pleased me,
I fed my cat by yonder tree;
  Cat goes fiddle-i-fee.

I had a hen and the hen pleased me,
I fed my hen by yonder tree;
        Hen goes chimmy-chuck,
           chimmy-chuck,
            Cat goes fiddle-i-fee.

I had a duck and the duck pleased me,
I fed my duck by yonder tree;
  Duck goes quack, quack,
  Hen goes chimmy-chuck, chimmy-chuck,
  Cat goes fiddle-i-fee.

I had a goose and the goose pleased me,
I fed my goose by yonder tree;
  Goose goes swishy, swashy,
  Duck goes quack, quack,
  Hen goes chimmy-chuck, chimmy-chuck,
  Cat goes fiddle-i-fee.

I had a sheep and the sheep pleased me,
I fed my sheep by yonder tree;
  Sheep goes baa, baa,
  Goose goes swishy, swashy,
  Duck goes quack, quack,
  Hen goes chimmy-chuck, chimmy-chuck,
  Cat goes fiddle-i-fee.

I had a pig and the pig pleased me,
I fed my pig by yonder tree;
  Pig goes griffy, gruffy,
  Sheep goes baa, baa,
  Goose goes swishy, swashy,
  Duck goes quack, quack,
  Hen goes chimmy-chuck, chimmy-chuck,
  Cat goes fiddle-i-fee.

I had a cow and the cow pleased me,
I fed my cow by yonder tree;
  Cow goes moo, moo,
  Pig goes griffy, gruffy,
  Sheep goes baa, baa,
  Goose goes swishy, swashy,
  Duck goes quack, quack,
  Hen goes chimmy-chuck, chimmy-chuck,
  Cat goes fiddle-i-fee.

I had a horse and the horse pleased me,
I fed my horse by yonder tree;
  Horse goes neigh, neigh,
  Cow goes moo, moo,
  Pig goes griffy, gruffy,
  Sheep goes baa, baa,
  Goose goes swishy, swashy,
  Duck goes quack, quack,
  Hen goes chimmy-chuck, chimmy-chuck,
  Cat goes fiddle-i-fee.

I had a dog and the dog pleased me,
I fed my dog by yonder tree;
  Dog goes bow-wow, bow-wow,
  Horse goes neigh, neigh,
  Cow goes moo, moo,
  Pig goes griffy, gruffy,
  Sheep goes baa, baa,
  Goose goes swishy, swashy,
  Duck goes quack, quack,
  Hen goes chimmy-chuck, chimmy-chuck,
  Cat goes fiddle-i-fee.

THE BELLS OF LONDON

Gay go up and gay go down,
To ring the bells of London town.

Halfpence and farthings,
Say the bells of St. Martin's.

Oranges and lemons,
Say the bells of St. Clement's.

Pancakes and fritters,
Say the bells of St. Peter's.

Two sticks and an apple,
Say the bells of Whitechapel.

Kettles and pans,
Say the bells of St. Ann's.

You owe me ten shillings,
Say the bells of St. Helen's.

When will you pay me?
Say the bells of Old Bailey.

When I grow rich,
Say the bells of Shoreditch.

Pray when will that be?
Say the bells of Stepney.

I am sure I don't know,
Says the great bell of Bow.

HOW MANY DAYS HAS MY BABY TO PLAY?

How many days has my baby to play?
Saturday, Sunday, Monday;
Tuesday, Wednesday, Thursday, Friday,
Saturday, Sunday, Monday.

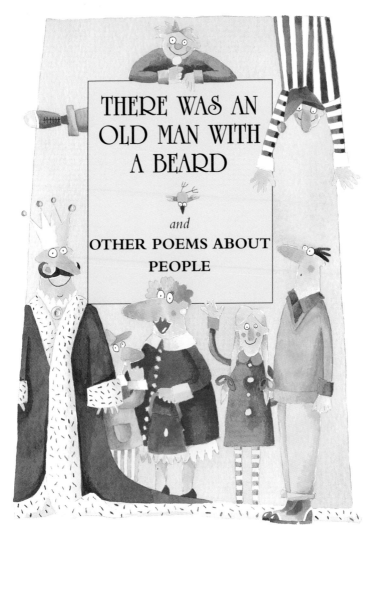

THERE WAS AN
OLD MAN WITH
A BEARD

and

OTHER POEMS ABOUT
PEOPLE

THERE WAS AN OLD MAN WITH A BEARD

There was an old Man with a beard,
Who said, "It is just as I feared!—
Two Owls and a Hen, four Larks and a Wren
Have all built their nests in my beard!"

EDWARD LEAR

OZYMANDIAS

I met a traveller from an antique land
Who said: Two vast and trunkless legs
    of stone
Stand in the desert....Near them, on the sand,
Half sunk, a shattered visage lies, whose
    frown,
And wrinkled lip, and sneer of cold command,
Tell that its sculptor well those passions read
Which yet survive, stamped on these
    lifeless things,
The hand that mocked them, and the
    heart that fed:

And on the pedestal these words appear:
"My name is Ozymandias, king of kings:
Look on my works, ye Mighty, and despair!"
Nothing beside remains. Round the decay
Of that colossal wreck, boundless and bare
The lone and level sands stretch far away.

PERCY BYSSHE SHELLEY

I EAT MY PEAS WITH HONEY

I eat my peas with honey,
I've done it all my life,
It makes the peas taste funny,
But it keeps them on my knife.

ANONYMOUS
AMERICAN

SEE A PIN AND PICK IT UP

See a pin and pick it up,
All the day you'll have good luck;
See a pin and let it lay,
Bad luck you'll have all the day!

BARBARA FRIETCHIE

Up from the meadows rich with corn,
Clear in the cool September morn,

The clustered spires of Frederick stand
Green-walled by the hills of Maryland.

Round about them orchards sweep,
Apple and peach tree fruited deep,

Fair as the garden of the Lord
To the eyes of the famished rebel horde,

On that pleasant morn of the early fall
When Lee marched over the mountain-wall;

Over the mountains winding down,
Horse and foot, into Frederick town.

Forty flags with their silver stars,
Forty flags with their crimson bars,

Flapped in the morning wind: the sun
Of noon looked down, and saw not one.

Up rose old Barbara Frietchie then,
Bowed with her fourscore years and ten;

Bravest of all in Frederick town,
She took up the flag the men hauled down,

In her attic window the staff she set,
To show that one heart was loyal yet.

Up the street came the rebel tread,
Stonewall Jackson riding ahead.

Under his slouched hat left and right
He glanced; the old flag met his sight.

"Halt!"—the dust-brown ranks stood fast.
"Fire!"—out blazed the rifle blast.

It shivered the window, pane and sash;
It rent the banner with seam and gash.

Quick, as it fell, from the broken staff
Dame Barbara snatched the silken scarf.

She leaned far out on the window-sill,
And shook it forth with a royal will.

"Shoot, if you must, this old gray head,
But spare your country's flag," she said.

A shade of sadness, a blush of shame,
Over the face of the leader came;

The nobler nature within him stirred
To life at that woman's deed and word;

"Who touches a hair of yon gray head
Dies like a dog! March on!" he said.

All day long through Frederick street
Sounded the tread of marching feet:

All day long that free flag tost
Over the heads of the rebel host.

Ever its torn folds rose and fell
On the loyal winds that loved it well;

And through the hill-gaps sunset light
Shone over it with a warm good-night.

Barbara Frietchie's work is o'er,
And the Rebel rides on his raids no more.

Peace and order and beauty draw
Round thy symbol of light and law;

And ever the stars above look down
On thy stars below in Frederick town!

Honor to her! and let a tear
Fall, for her sake, on Stonewall's bier.

Over Barbara Frietchie's grave,
Flag of Freedom and Union, wave!

JOHN GREENLEAF WHITTIER

MEG MERRILEES

Old Meg she was a Gipsy,
  And lived upon the moors:
Her bed it was the brown heath turf,
  And her house was out of doors.

Her apples were swart blackberries,
  Her currants pods o'broom;
Her wind was dew of the wild white rose,
  Her book a churchyard tomb.

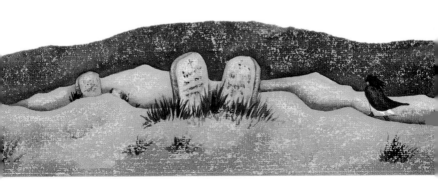

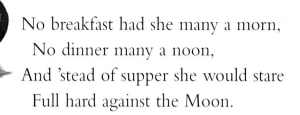

No breakfast had she many a morn,
  No dinner many a noon,
And 'stead of supper she would stare
  Full hard against the Moon.

But every morn of woodbine fresh
  She made her garlanding,
And every night the dark glen Yew
  She wove, and she would sing.

And with her fingers, old and brown,
  She plaited Mats o' Rushes,
And gave them to the Cottagers
  She met among the Bushes.

Old Meg was brave as Margaret Queen,
  And tall as Amazon;
An old red blanket cloak she wore;
  A chip hat had she on.
God rest her aged bones somewhere—
  She died full long agone!

JOHN KEATS

THE AKOND OF SWAT

Who or why, or which, or *what,*
    Is the Akond of SWAT?

Is he tall or short, or dark or fair?
Does he sit on a stool or a sofa or chair,
    or SQUAT,

              The Akond of Swat?

Is he wise or foolish, young or old?
Does he drink his soup and his coffee cold,
    or HOT,

                   The Akond of Swat?

Does he sing or whistle, jabber or talk,
And when riding abroad does he gallop or walk,
    or TROT,

                   The Akond of Swat?

Does he wear a turban, a fez, or a hat?
Does he sleep on a mattress, a bed, or a mat,
    or a COT,

                The Akond of Swat?

When he writes a copy in round-hand size,
Does he cross his T's and finish his I's with
    a DOT,

                The Akond of Swat?

Can he write a letter concisely clear
Without a speck or a smudge or a
    smear or BLOT,

                The Akond of Swat?

Do his people like him extremely well?
Or do they, whenever they can, rebel,
    or PLOT,

                At the Akond of Swat?

If he catches them then, either old or young,
Does he have them chopped in pieces or
   hung, or SHOT,
               The Akond of Swat?

Do his people prig in the lanes or park,
Or even at times, when days are dark,
   GAROTTE?
               O the Akond of Swat!

Does he study the wants of his own dominion?
Or doesn't he care for public opinion a JOT,
               The Akond of Swat?

To amuse his mind do his people show him
Pictures, or any one's last new poem,
   or WHAT,
               For the Akond of Swat?

At night if he suddenly screams and wakes,
Do they bring him only a few small cakes,
 or a LOT,

 For the Akond of Swat?

Does he live on turnips, tea, or tripe?
Does he like his shawl to be marked with a stripe,
 or a DOT,

 The Akond of Swat?

Does he like to lie on his back in a boat
Like the lady who lived in that isle remote,
 SHALLOTT,

 The Akond of Swat?

Is he quiet, or always making a fuss?
Is his steward a Swiss or a Swede or a Russ,
 or a SCOT,

 The Akond of Swat?

Does he like to sit by the calm blue wave?
Or to sleep and snore in a dark green cave,
   or a GROTT,

          The Akond of Swat?

Does he drink small beer from a silver jug?
Or a bowl? or a glass? or a cup? or a mug?
   or a POT,

          The Akond of Swat?

Does be beat his wife with a gold-topped pipe,
When she lets the gooseberries grow too ripe,
   or ROT,
   The Akond of Swat?

Does he wear a white tie when dining with friends,
And tie it neat in a bow with ends, or a KNOT,
                    The Akond of Swat?

Does he like new cream, and hate mince-pies?
When he looks at the sun does he wink his eyes,
  or NOT,

                    The Akond of Swat?

Does he teach his subjects to roast and bake?
Does he sail about on an inland lake, in a YACHT,
                    The Akond of Swat?

Some one, or nobody, knows I wot
Who or which or why or what
                    Is the Akond of Swat!

EDWARD LEAR

THREE WISE OLD WOMEN

Three wise old women were they,
   were they,
Who went to walk on a winter day:
One carried a basket to hold some berries,
One carried a ladder to climb for cherries,
The third, and she was the wisest one,
Carried a fan to keep off the sun.

But they went so far, and they went so fast,
They quite forgot their way at last,
So one of the wise women cried in a fright,
"Suppose we should meet a bear tonight!
Suppose he should eat me!" "And me!!"
"And me!!!"
"What is to be done?" cried all the three.

"Dear, dear!" said one, "we'll climb a tree,
There out of the way of the bears we'll be."
But there wasn't a tree for miles around;
They were too frightened to stay on
    the ground,
So they climbed their ladder up to the top,
And sat there screaming "We'll drop!
    We'll drop!"

But the wind was strong as wind could be,
And blew their ladder right out to sea;
So the three wise women were all afloat
In a leaky ladder instead of a boat,
And every time the waves rolled in,
Of course the poor things were wet to
    the skin.

Then they took their basket, the water
    to bale,
They put up their fan instead of a sail:
But what became of the wise
    women then,
Whether they ever sailed home again,
Whether they saw any bears, or no,
You must find out, for I don't know.

ELIZABETH T. CORBETT

MY MOTHER

Who fed me from her gentle breast,
And hushed me in her arms to rest,
And on my cheek sweet kisses prest?
      My Mother.

When sleep forsook my open eye,
Who was it sung sweet hushaby,
And rocked me that I should not cry?
      My Mother.

Who sat and watched my
  infant head,
When sleeping on my
  cradle bed,
And tears of sweet
  affection shed?
      My Mother.

When pain and sickness made my cry,
Who gazed upon my heavy eye,
And wept, for fear that I should die?
My Mother.

Who dressed my doll in clothes so gay,
And fondly taught me how to play,
And minded all I have to say?
My Mother.

Who ran to help me when I fell,
And would some pretty
story tell,
Or kiss the place to make it well?
My Mother.

Who taught my infant lips to pray,
And love God's holy book and day,
And walk in wisdom's
  pleasant way?
                My Mother.

And can I ever cease to be
Affectionate and kind to thee,
Who was so very kind to me,
                My Mother?

Ah no! the thought I cannot bear,
And if God please my life to spare,
I hope I shall reward thy care,
                My Mother.

When thou are feeble, old, and grey,
My healthy arm shall be thy stay,
And I will soothe thy pains away,
          My Mother.

And when I see thee hang thy head,
'Twill be my turn to watch thy bed,
And tears of sweet affection shed,
          My Mother.

For could our Father in the skies
Look down with pleased or loving eyes,
If ever I could dare despise
          My Mother?

ANN TAYLOR

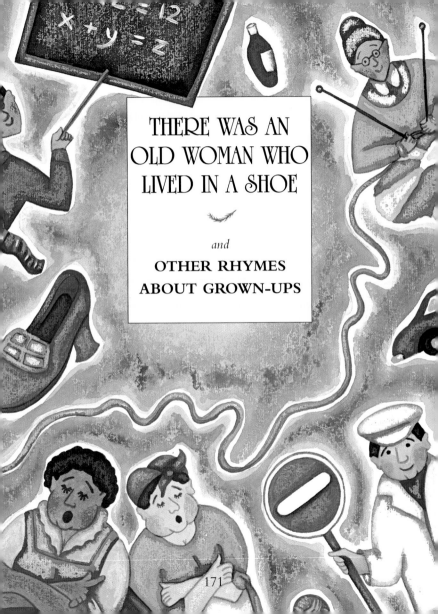

THERE WAS AN OLD WOMAN WHO LIVED IN A SHOE

and

OTHER RHYMES ABOUT GROWN-UPS

THERE WAS AN OLD WOMAN
WHO LIVED IN A SHOE

There was an old woman who lived in a shoe,
She had so many children she didn't know
 what to do;
She gave them some broth without any bread;
And scolded them soundly and put them to bed.

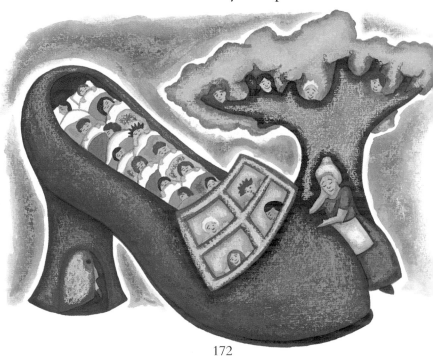

THERE WAS AN OLD WOMAN
WENT UP IN A BASKET

There was an old woman went up in a basket,
Seventy times as high as the moon;
What she did there I could not but ask it,
For in her hand she carried a broom.
"Old woman, old woman, old woman," said I,
"Whither oh whither oh whither so high?"
"To sweep the cobwebs from the sky,
And I shall be back again by and by."

ONE MISTY MOISTY MORNING

One misty moisty morning,
When cloudy was the weather,
There I met an old man
Clothed all in leather;

Clothed all in leather,
With cap under his chin—
How do you do, and how do you do,
And how do you do again!

THERE WAS A CROOKED MAN

There was a crooked man, and he went a
  crooked mile,
He found a crooked sixpence against a
  crooked stile;
He bought a crooked cat, which caught a
  crooked mouse,
And they all lived together in a little crooked house.

OLD MOTHER HUBBARD

Old Mother Hubbard
  Went to the cupboard
  To get her poor dog a bone;
But when she came there
The cupboard was bare,
  And so the poor dog had none.

She went to the baker's
  To buy him some bread,
But when she came back
  The poor dog was dead.

She went to the joiner's
  To buy him a coffin,
But when she came back
  The poor dog was laughing.

She took a clean dish
  To get him some tripe,
But when she came back
  He was smoking his pipe.

She went to the fishmonger's
  To buy him some fish,
And when she came back
  He was licking the dish.

She went to the ale-house
  To get him some beer,
But when she came back
  The dog sat in a chair.

She went to the tavern
  For white wine and red,
But when she came back
  The dog stood on his head.

She went to the hatter's
  To buy him a hat,
But when she came back
  He was feeding the cat.

She went to the barber's
　　To buy him a wig,
But when she came back
　　He was dancing a jig.

She went to the fruiterer's
　　To buy him some fruit,
But when she came back
　　He was playing the flute.

She went to the tailor's
  To buy him a coat,
But when she came back
  He was riding a goat.

She went to the cobbler's
  To buy him some shoes,
But when she came back
  He was reading the news.

She went to the sempstress
To buy him some linen,
But when she came back
The dog was spinning.

She went to the hosier's
To buy him some hose,
But when she came back
He was dressed in his clothes.

The dame made a curtsey,
The dog made a bow;
The dame said, "Your servant,"
The dog said, "Bow, wow."

RUB-A-DUB DUB

Rub-a-dub dub,
Three men in a tub,
And who do you think they be?
The butcher, the baker,
The candle-stick maker,
And they all jumped out of a rotten potato.

DOCTOR FOSTER WENT TO GLOUCESTER

Doctor Foster went to Gloucester,
  In a shower of rain;
He stepped in a puddle, up to his middle,
  And never went there again.

AS I WALKED BY MYSELF

As I walked by myself,
And talked to myself,
  Myself said unto me,
Look to thyself,
Take care of thyself,
  For nobody cares for thee.

I answered myself,
And said to myself,
  In the self-same repartee,
Look to thyself,
Or not look to thyself,
  The self-same thing will be.

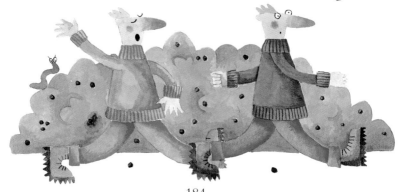

IT'S RAINING, IT'S POURING

It's raining, it's pouring,
The old man is snoring;
He went to bed and bumped his head
And couldn't get up in the morning.

THERE WAS A KING, AND HE HAD THREE DAUGHTERS

There was a king, and he had three daughters,
And they all lived in a basin of water;
  The basin bended,
  My story's ended.
If the basin had been stronger,
My story would have been longer.

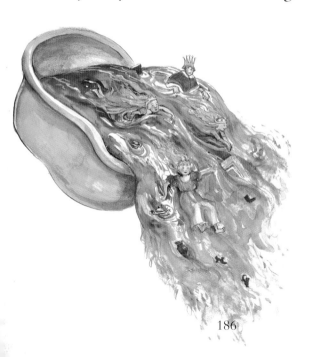

THE FAIRIES

and
OTHER MAGICAL
POEMS

THE FAIRIES

Up the airy mountain,
Down the rushy glen,
We daren't go a-hunting
For fear of little men;
Wee folk, good folk,
Trooping all together;
Green jacket, red cap,
And white owl's feather!

Down along the rocky shore
  Some make their home;
They live on crispy pancakes
  Of yellow tide-foam;
Some in the reeds
  Of the black mountain lake,
With frogs for their watch-dogs,
  All night awake.

High on the hill-top
  The old King sits;
He is now so old and grey
  He's nigh lost his wits.
With a bridge of white mist
  Columbkill he crosses,

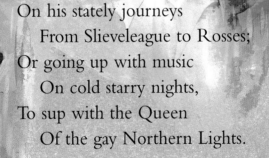

On his stately journeys
    From Slieveleague to Rosses;
Or going up with music
    On cold starry nights,
To sup with the Queen
    Of the gay Northern Lights.

They stole little Bridget
  For seven years long;
When she came down again,
  Her friends were all gone.
They took her lightly back,
  Between the night and morrow,
They thought that she was fast
    asleep,
  But she was dead with sorrow.
They have kept her ever since
  Deep within the lake,
On a bed of flag-leaves,
  Watching till she wake.

By the craggy hill-side,
  Through the mosses bare,
They have planted thorn-trees
  For pleasure here and there.

Is any man so daring
    As dig them up in spite,
He shall find the thornies set
    In his bed at night.

Up the airy mountain,
    Down the rushy glen,
We daren't go a-hunting
    For fear of little men;
Wee folk, good folk,
    Trooping all together;
Green jacket, red cap,
    And white owl's feather!

WILLIAM ALLINGHAM

THE MAD GARDENER'S SONG

He thought he saw an Elephant,
  That practised on a fife;
He looked again, and found it was
  A letter from his wife.
"At length I realize," he said,
  "The bitterness of Life!"

He thought he saw a Buffalo
Upon the chimney-piece:
He looked again, and found it was
His Sister's Husband's Niece.
"Unless you leave this house," he said,
"I'll send for the Police!"

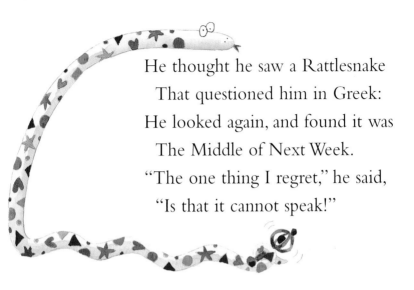

He thought he saw a Rattlesnake
That questioned him in Greek:
He looked again, and found it was
The Middle of Next Week.
"The one thing I regret," he said,
"Is that it cannot speak!"

He thought he saw a Banker's Clerk
Descending from the bus:
He looked again, and found it was
A Hippopotamus:
"If this should stay to dine," he said,
"There won't be much for us!"

He thought he saw a Kangaroo
  That worked a coffee-mill:
He looked again, and found it was
  A Vegetable-Pill.
"Were I to swallow this," he said,
  "I should be very ill!"

He thought he saw a Coach-and-Four
  That stood beside his bed:
He looked again, and found it was
  A Bear without a Head.
"Poor thing," he said, "poor silly thing!
  It's waiting to be fed!"

He thought he saw an Albatross
  That fluttered round the lamp:
He looked again, and found it was
  A Penny-Postage-Stamp.
"You'd best be getting home," he said,
  "The nights are very damp!"

He thought he saw a Garden-Door
  That opened with a key:
He looked again, and found it was
  A Double Rule of Three:
"And all its mystery," he said,
  "Is clear as day to me!"

He thought he saw an Argument
That proved he was the Pope:
He look again, and found it was
A Bar of Mottled Soap.
"A fact so dread," he faintly said,
"Extinguishes all hope!"

LEWIS CARROLL

KUBLA KHAN

In Xanadu did Kubla Khan
  A stately pleasure-dome decree;
Where Alph, the sacred river, ran
Through caverns measureless to man
  Down to a sunless sea.

So twice five miles of fertile ground
With walls and towers were girdled round;
And here were gardens bright with sinuous rills
Where blossomed many an incense-bearing tree;
And here were forests ancient as the hills,
Enfolding sunny spots of greenery.

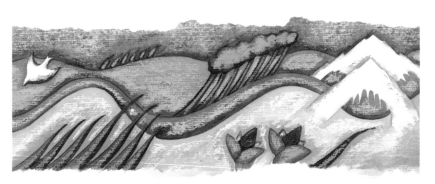

But O, that deep romantic chasm which slanted
Down the green hill athwart a cedarn cover!
A savage place! as holy and enchanted
As e'er beneath a waning moon was haunted
By woman wailing for her demon-lover!
And from this chasm, with ceaseless turmoil seething,
As if this earth in fast thick pants were breathing,
A mighty fountain momently was forced;
Amid whose swift half-intermitted burst
Huge fragments vaulted like rebounding hail,
Or chaffy grain beneath the thresher's flail:
And 'mid these dancing rocks at once and ever:

It flung up momently the sacred river,
Five miles meandering with a mazy motion
Through wood and dale the sacred river ran,
Then reached the caverns measureless to man
And sank in tumult to a lifeless ocean:
And 'mid this tumult Kubla heard from far
Ancestral voices prophesying war!

The shadow of the dome of pleasure
Floated midway on the waves;
Where was heard the mingled measure
From the fountain and the caves.

It was a miracle of rare device,
A sunny pleasure-dome with caves
  of ice!

A damsel with a dulcimer
In a vision once I saw:
It was an Abyssinian maid,
And on her dulcimer she played,
Singing of Mount Abora.
Could I revive within me
Her symphony and song,
To such a deep delight 'twould win me,

That with music loud and long,
I would build that dome in air,
That sunny dome! those caves of ice!
And all who heard should see them
    there,
And all should cry, Beware! Beware!
His flashing eyes, his floating hair!
Weave a circle round him thrice,
And close your eyes with holy dread,
For he on honey-dew hath fed,
And drunk the milk of Paradise.

SAMUEL TAYLOR COLERIDGE

THE BUTTERFLY'S BALL

Come take up your hats, and away let us haste,
To the Butterfly's Ball, and the Grasshopper's Feast.
The trumpeter Gadfly has summoned the crew,
And the revels are now only waiting for you.

On the smooth-shaven grass by the side of a wood,
Beneath a broad oak which for ages has stood,
See the children of earth and the tenants of air,
For an evening's amusement together repair.

And there came the Beetle, so blind and so black,
Who carried the Emmet, his friend, on his back.
And there came the Gnat, and the Dragonfly too,
And all their relations, green, orange, and blue.

And there came the Moth, with her plumage of down,
And the Hornet, with jacket of yellow and brown;
Who with him the Wasp, his companion, did bring,
But they promised that evening, to lay by their sting.

Then the sly little Dormouse crept out of his hole,
And led to the feast his blind cousin the Mole.
And the Snail, with his horns peeping out of his shell,
Came, fatigued with the distance, the length of an ell.

A mushroom their table, and on it was laid
A water-dock leaf, which a tablecloth made.
The viands were various, to each of their taste,
And the Bee brought the honey to sweeten the feast.

With steps most majestic the Snail did advance,
And he promised the gazers a minuet to dance;
But they all laughed so loud that he drew in
   his head,
And went in his own little chamber to bed.

Then, as evening gave way to the shadows of night,
Their watchman, the Glow-worm, came out
   with his light.
So home let us hasten, while yet we can see;
For no watchman is waiting for you and for me.

WILLIAM ROSCOE

MY MOTHER SAID

My mother said, I never should
Play with gypsies in the wood.

If I did, then she would say:
"Naughty girl to disobey!

"Your hair shan't curl and your
  shoes shan't shine,
You gypsy girl, you shan't be mine!"

And my father said that if I did,
He'd rap my head with the teapot-lid.

My mother said that I never should
Play with the gypsies in the wood.

The wood was dark, the grass
   was green;
By came Sally with a tambourine.

I went to sea—no ship to get across;
I paid ten shillings for a blind
   white horse.

I upped on his back and was off in
   a crack,
Sally tell my mother I shall never
   come back.

ANONYMOUS

ENGLISH

ROUND AND ROUND THE GARDEN

and

OTHER ACTION RHYMES, TONGUE-TWISTERS, AND RIDDLES

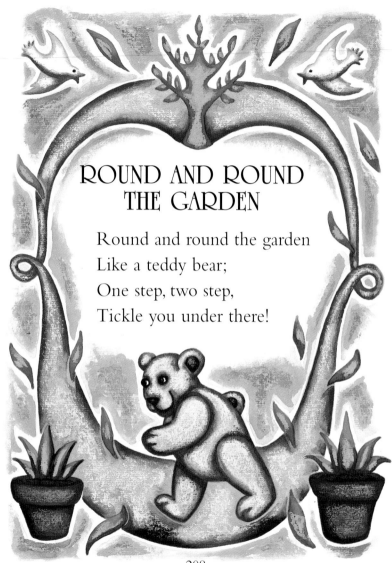

ROUND AND ROUND
THE GARDEN

Round and round the garden
Like a teddy bear;
One step, two step,
Tickle you under there!

MY GRANDMOTHER SENT ME

My grandmother sent me a new-fashioned three
cornered cambric country cut handkerchief.
Not an old-fashioned three cornered
cambric country cut handkerchief,
but a new-fashioned
three cornered cambric
country cut
handkerchief.

ROBERT ROWLEY

Robert Rowley rolled a round roll round,
A round roll Robert Rowley rolled round;
Where rolled the round roll
Robert Rowley rolled round?

LEG OVER LEG

Leg over leg,
   As the dog went to Dover;
      When he came to a stile,
         Jump he went over.

THE SHORTEST
TONGUE-TWISTER

Peggy Babcock

I WENT UP ONE PAIR OF STAIRS

FOR TWO VOICES

I went up one pair of stairs.
  Just like me.
I went up two pairs of stairs.
  Just like me.
I went into a room.
  Just like me.
I looked out of a window.
  Just like me.
And there I saw a monkey.
  Just like me.

211

MY MOTHER AND YOUR MOTHER

My mother and your mother
  Went over the way;
Said my mother to your mother,
  It's chop-a-nose day!

A FACE GAME

Here sits the Lord Mayor;   *Forehead*
  Here sit his two men;   *Eyes*
Here sits the cock;   *Right cheek*
  Here sits the hen;   *Left cheek*
Here sit the little chickens; *Tip of nose*
  Here they run in,   *Mouth*
Chinchopper, chinchopper,
  Chinchopper, chin!   *Chuck the chin*

THE
DARK
WOOD

In the dark, dark wood, there was
 a dark, dark house,
And in that dark, dark house, there was
 a dark, dark room,
And in that dark, dark room, there was
 a dark, dark cupboard,
And in that dark, dark cupboard, there was
 a dark, dark shelf,
And on that dark, dark shelf, there was
 a dark, dark box,
And in that dark, dark box,
 there was a
 GHOST!

I MET A MAN

As I was going up the stair
I met a man who wasn't there.
He wasn't there again today—
Oh! how I wish he'd go away!

ADAM AND EVE AND PINCHME

Adam and Eve and Pinchme
Went down to the river to bathe.
Adam and Eve were drowned—
Who do you think was saved?

PETER PIPER

Peter Piper picked a peck of pickled pepper;
A peck of pickled pepper Peter Piper picked;
If Peter Piper picked a peck of pickled pepper,
Where's the peck of pickled pepper
Peter Piper picked?

RIDE A COCK-HORSE

Ride a cock-horse to Banbury Cross,
  To see a fine lady ride on a white horse,
Rings on her fingers and bells on her toes,
  She shall have music wherever she goes.

SWAN SWAM OVER THE SEA

Swan swam over the sea—
Swim, swan, swim,
Swan swam back again,
Well swum swan.

HEY, DOROLOT, DOROLOT!

Hey, dorolot, dorolot!
Hey, dorolay, dorolay!
Hey, my bonny boat, bonny boat,
Hey, drag away, drag away!

TEDDY BEAR, TEDDY BEAR

Teddy bear, teddy bear,
Turn around.
Teddy bear, teddy bear,
Touch the ground.
Teddy bear, teddy bear,
Show your shoe.
Teddy bear, teddy bear,
That will do.

Teddy bear, teddy bear,
Go upstairs.
Teddy bear, teddy bear,
Say your prayers.
Teddy bear, teddy bear,
Turn out the light.
Teddy bear, teddy bear,
Say good night.

ONE, TWO, THREE, FOUR, FIVE

One, two, three, four, five,
  I caught a fish alive;
Six, seven, eight, nine, ten,
  I let him go again.
Why did you let him go?
  Because he bit my finger so.
Which little finger did he bight?
  This little finger on the right.

THIS LITTLE PIGGY

This little piggy went to market,
This little piggy stayed at home,
This little piggy had roast beef,
This little piggy had none,
And this little piggy cried, *Wee-wee-wee-wee-wee,*
  All the way home.

THIS IS THE WAY THE LADIES RIDE

This is the way the ladies ride:
  Tri, tre, tre, tree,
  Tri, tre, tre, tree!
This is the way the ladies ride:
  Tri, tre, tre, tre, tri-tre-tre-tree!

This is the way the gentlemen ride:
  Gallop-a-trot,
  Gallop-a-trot!
This is the way the gentlemen ride:
  Gallop-a-gallop-a-trot!

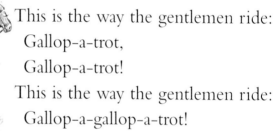

This is the way the farmers ride:
  Hobbledy-hoy,
  Hobbledy-hoy!
This is the way the farmers ride:
  Hobbledy hobbledy-hoy!

ME, MYSELF, AND I

Me, myself, and I—
We went to the kitchen and ate a pie.
Then my mother she came in
And chased us out with a rolling pin.

MICHAEL FINNEGAN

There was an old man called Michael Finnegan
He grew whiskers on his chinnegan
The wind came out and blew them in again
Poor old Michael Finnegan. *Begin again...*

HUSH
LITTLE BABY

and

OTHER
BEDTIME POEMS

HUSH, LITTLE BABY

Hush, little baby, don't say a word,
Papa's going to buy you a mocking bird.

If the mocking bird won't sing,
Papa's going to buy you a diamond ring.

If the diamond ring turn to brass,
Papa's going to buy you a looking-glass.

If the looking-glass gets broke,
Papa's going to buy you a billy-goat.

If that billy-goat runs away,
Papa's going to buy you another today.

ANONYMOUS
AMERICAN

228

THE MOUSE'S LULLABY

Oh, rock-a-by, baby mouse, rock-a-by, so!
When baby's asleep to the baker's I'll go,
And while he's not looking I'll pop from a hole,
And bring to my baby a fresh penny roll.

PALMER COX

NIGHT

The sun descending in the west,
The evening star does shine;
The birds are silent in their nest,
And I must seek for mine.
  The moon, like a flower,
  In heaven's high bower,
  With silent delight
  Sits and smiles on the night.

  Farewell, green fields and happy groves,
  Where flocks have took delight;
  Where lambs have nibbled, silent moves
  The feet of angels bright;
    Unseen they pour blessing,
    And joy without ceasing,
    On each bud and blossom,
    And each sleeping bosom.

They look in every thoughtless nest,
Where birds are covered warm;
They visit caves of every beast,
To keep them all from harm.
  If they see any weeping,
  That should have been sleeping,
  They pour sleep on their head,
  And sit down by their bed.

When wolves and tigers howl for prey,
They pitying stand and weep;
Seeking to drive their thirst away,
And keep them from the sheep.
  But if they rush dreadful,
  The angels, most heedful,
  Receive each mild spirit,
  New worlds to inherit.

And there the lion's ruddy eyes
Shall flow with tears of gold,
And pitying the tender cries,
And walking round the fold,
　　Saying, "Wrath, by his meekness,
　　And, by his health, sickness
　　Is driven away
　　From our immortal day.

　　"And now beside thee, bleating lamb,
　　I can lie down and sleep;
　　Or think on him who bore thy name,
　　Graze after thee and weep.
　　　　For, washed in life's river,
　　　　My bright mane for ever
　　　　Shall shine like the gold,
　　　　As I guard o'er the fold."

WILLIAM BLAKE

BED IN SUMMER

In winter I get up at night
And dress by yellow candle-light.
In summer, quite the other way,
I have to go to bed by day.

I have to go to bed and see
The birds still hopping on the tree,
Or hear the grown-up people's feet
Still going past me in the street.

And does it not seem hard to you,
When all the sky is clear and blue,
And I should like so much to play,
To have to go to bed by day?

ROBERT LOUIS STEVENSON

ROCK-A-BYE, BABY

Rock-a-bye, baby, thy cradle is green;
Father's a nobleman, Mother's a queen,
And Betty's a lady, and wears a gold ring,
And Johnny's a drummer, and drums for the King.

BYE, BABY BUNTING

Bye, baby bunting,
Father's gone a-hunting,
To fetch a little rabbit-skin
To wrap his baby bunting in.

IN THE TREE-TOP

"Rock-a-by, baby, up in the tree-top!"
    Mother his blanket is spinning;
And a light little rustle that never
    will stop,
    Breezes and boughs are beginning.
Rock-a-by, baby, swinging so high!
        Rock-a-by!

"When the wind blows, then the
    cradle will rock."
    Hush! now it stirs in the bushes;
Now with a whisper, a flutter of talk,
    Baby and hammock it pushes.
Rock-a-by, baby! shut, pretty eye!
        Rock-a-by!

"Rock with the boughs, rock-a-by, baby dear!"
  Leaf-tongues are singing and saying;
Mother she listens, and sister is near,
  Under the tree softly playing.
Rock-a-by, baby! mother's close by!
      Rock-a-by!

Weave him a beautiful dream, little breeze!
  Little leaves, nestle around him!
He will remember the song of the trees,
  When age with silver has crowned him.
Rock-a-by, baby!
wake by-and-by!
Rock-a-by!

LUCY LARCOM

NOW THE DAY IS OVER

Now the day is over,
  Night is drawing nigh,
Shadows of the evening
  Steal across the sky.

Now the darkness gathers,
  Stars begin to peep,
Birds and beasts and flowers
  Soon will be asleep.

Jesu, give the weary
  Calm and sweet repose;
With thy tenderest blessing
  May our eyelids close.

Grant to little children
  Visions bright of thee;
Guard the sailors tossing
  On the deep blue sea.

Comfort every sufferer
  Watching late in pain;
Those who plan some evil
  From their sin restrain.

Through the long night-watches
  May thine angels spread
Their white wings above me,
  Watching round my bed.

When the morning wakens,
  Then may I arise
Pure and fresh and sinless
  In thy holy eyes.

Glory to the Father,
  Glory to the son,
And to thee, blest Spirit,
  Whilst all ages run.

SABINE BARING-GOULD

A CRADLE SONG

Golden slumbers kiss your eyes,
Smiles awake you when you rise.
Sleep, pretty wantons, do not cry,
And I will sing a lullaby:
Rock them, rock them, lullaby.

Care is heavy, therefore sleep you;
You are care, and care must keep you.
Sleep, pretty wantons, do not cry,
And I will sing a lullaby:
Rock them, rock them, lullaby.

THOMAS DEKKER

SIMPLE GIFTS

and

OTHER POEMS TO
MAKE YOU THINK

SIMPLE GIFTS

'Tis the gift to be simple,
'Tis the gift to be free,
'Tis the gift to come down
Where we ought to be,
And when we find ourselves
In the place just right,
'Twill be in the valley
Of love and delight.
When true simplicity is gained
To bow and to bend
We sha'n't be ashamed,
To turn, turn will be our delight,
Till by turning, turning
We come round right.

ANONYMOUS
AMERICAN, SHAKER SONG

LITTLE THINGS

Little drops of water,
　Little grains of sand,
Make the mighty ocean
　And the beauteous land.

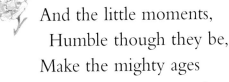

And the little moments,
　Humble though they be,
Make the mighty ages
　Of eternity.

So our little errors
　Lead the soul away,
From the paths of virtue
　Into sin to stray.

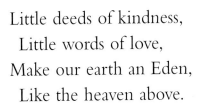

Little deeds of kindness,
　Little words of love,
Make our earth an Eden,
　Like the heaven above.

JULIA A. CARNEY

A BABY-SERMON

The lightning and thunder
  They go and they come;
But the stars and the stillness
  Are always at home.

GEORGE MACDONALD

WAGTAIL AND BABY

A baby watched a ford, whereto
  A wagtail came for drinking;
A blaring bull went wading through,
  The wagtail showed no shrinking.

A stallion splashed his way across,
  The birdie nearly sinking;
He gave his plumes a twitch and toss,
  And held his own unblinking.

Next saw the baby round the spot
  A mongrel slowing slinking;
The wagtail gazed, but faltered not
  In dip and sip and prinking.

A perfect gentleman then neared;
  The wagtail, in a winking,
With terror rose and disappeared;
  The baby fell a-thinking.

THOMAS HARDY

MY SHADOW

I have a little shadow that goes in and out with me,
And what can be the use of him is more than I can see.
He is very, very like me from the heels up to the head;
And I see him jump before me,
  when I jump into my bed.

The funniest thing about him is the way he likes
  to grow—
Not at all like proper children, which is always
  very slow;
For he sometimes shoots up taller like
  an india-rubber ball,
And he sometimes
  gets so little that
  there's none of
  him at all.

He hasn't got a notion of how children ought to play,
And can only make a fool of me in every sort of way.
He stays so close beside me, he's a coward you can see;
I'd think shame to stick to nursie
  as that shadow sticks to me!

One morning, very early, before the sun was up,
I rose and found the shining dew on every buttercup;
  But my lazy little shadow, like an arrant sleepyhead,
    Had stayed at home behind me and was
        fast asleep in bed.

ROBERT LOUIS STEVENSON

LOVING AND LIKING

There's more in words that I can teach:
Yet listen, Child—I would not preach,
But only give some plain directions
To guide your speech and your affections.

Say not you LOVE a roasted fowl,
But you may love a screaming owl
And, if you can, the unwieldy toad
That crawls from his secure abode
Within the mossy garden wall
When evening dews begin to fall.

And when, upon some showery day,
Into a path or public way
A frog leaps out from bordering grass,
Startling the timid as they pass,
Do you observe him, and endeavour
To take the intruder into favour,
Learning from him to find a reason
For a light heart in a dull season.

The spring's first rose by you espied
May fill your breast with joyful pride;
And you may love the strawberry-flower,
And love the strawberry in its bower;
But when the fruit, so often praised
For beauty, to your lip is raised,

Say not you LOVE the delicate treat,
But LIKE it, enjoy it, and thankfully eat.
Long may you love your pensioner mouse,
Though one of a tribe that torment the house:
Nor dislike her cruel sport the cat,
Deadly foe both of mouse and rat.

Remember she follows the law of her kind,
And Instinct is neither wayward nor blind.
Then think of her beautiful gliding form,
Her tread that would scarcely crush a worm,
And her soothing song by the winter fire,
Soft as the dying throb of the lyre.
I would not circumscribe your love:

It may soar with the eagle and brood
    with the dove,
May pierce the earth with the patient mole,
Or track the hedgehog to his hole.
Loving and liking are the solace of life,
Rock the cradle of joy, smooth the death-bed
    of strife.
You love your father and your mother,
Your grown-up and your baby brother:
You love your sister, and your friends,
And countless blessings, which God sends:
    But LIKINGS come, and pass away:
        'Tis love that remains till our latest day.

DOROTHY WORDSWORTH

DON'T-CARE

Don't-care didn't care;
  Don't-care was wild.
Don't-care stole plum and pear
  Like any beggar's child.

Don't-care was made to care,
  Don't-care was hung:
Don't-care was put in the pot
  And boiled till he was done.

ANONYMOUS
ENGLISH

WHOLE DUTY OF CHILDREN

A child should always say what's true,
And speak when he is spoken to,
And behave mannerly at table:
At least as far as he is able.

ROBERT LOUIS STEVENSON

AGAINST QUARRELLING AND FIGHTING

Let dogs delight to bark and bite,
  For God hath made them so:
Let bears and lions growl and fight,
  For 'tis their nature, too.

But, children, you should never let
  Such angry passions rise:
Your little hands were never made
  To tear each other's eyes.

Let love through all your actions run,
  And all your words be mild:
Live like the blessed Virgin's Son,
  That sweet and lovely child.

His soul was gentle as a lamb;
  And as his nature grew,
He grew in favor both with man,
  And God his Father, too.

Now, Lord of all, he reigns above,
  And from his heavenly throne
He sees what children dwell in love,
  And marks them for his own.

Isaac Watts

THE WIND

Who has seen the wind?
  Neither I nor you;
But when the leaves hang trembling
  The wind is passing through.

Who has seen the wind?
  Neither you nor I;
But when the trees bow down their heads
  The wind is passing by.

CHRISTINA ROSSETTI